What's the Issue?

WHAT'S INFLATION?

By Donna Reynolds

KidHaven
PUBLISHING

Published in 2024 by
KidHaven Publishing, an Imprint of Greenhaven Publishing, LLC
2544 Clinton Street
Buffalo, NY 14224

Designer: Deanna Paternostro
Editor: Jennifer Lombardo

Photo credits: Cover (top) kurhan/Shutterstock.com; cover (bottom) Rawpixel.com/Shutterstock.com; p. 5 Seashell World/Shutterstock.com; p. 7 shisu_ka/Shutterstock.com; p. 9 Joseph Sohm/Shutterstock.com; p. 11 VectorMine/Shutterstock.com; p. 13 Foodio/Shutterstock.com; p. 15 Oleg Golovnev/Shutterstock.com; p. 17 Mila Supinskaya Glashchenko/Shutterstock.com; p. 19 Stephen Barnes/Shutterstock.com; p. 21 Audom/Shutterstock.com.

Library of Congress Cataloging-in-Publication Data

Names: Reynolds, Donna, author.
Title: What's inflation? / Donna Reynolds.
Description: Buffalo, NY : KidHaven Publishing, [2024] | Series: What's the issue? | Includes bibliographical references and index.
Identifiers: LCCN 2022049681 | ISBN 9781534544031 (library binding) | ISBN 9781534544024 (paperback) | ISBN 9781534544048 (ebook)
Subjects: LCSH: Inflation (Finance)–Juvenile literature. | Economics–Juvenile literature.
Classification: LCC HG229 .R49 2024 | DDC 332.4/1–dc23/eng/20221020
LC record available at https://lccn.loc.gov/2022049681

Printed in the United States of America

CPSIA compliance information: Batch #CSKH24: For further information contact Greenhaven Publishing LLC at 1-844-317-7404.

CONTENTS

Understanding the Economy

To understand inflation, it's helpful to know what an economy is. It's the way goods and services are produced and sold. In the past, many places had a **barter** economy. People would talk to each other about one good or service they would trade for another.

Around 11,000 years ago, people started using currency, or money. This can be anything people decide is **valuable**, including shells and livestock. Most money is now made of paper (banknotes) and metal (coins). People also use credit cards, but they need money in the bank to pay after using their card.

Facing the Facts

It's impossible to have inflation in a barter economy because people decide on what something is worth. Inflation can only happen in an economy that uses money.

The cowrie shell is the form of money that has been used the longest and in the most places in human history.

Money	Place Started	Year Started
livestock	global	9000–6000 BCE
cowrie shells	China, Africa	1200 BCE
silver coins	Turkey, Greece, Rome	500 BCE
leather squares	China	118 BCE
wampum	Native American groups	1535 CE
gold	England	1816 CE
Bitcoin (electronic money)	the internet	2009 CE

Agreeing to Pretend

The idea of money isn't something that comes from nature. Instead, it's something humans made up to make it easier to get goods and services. Money only works if we all agree that shells, pieces of paper, or numbers on a screen have value.

However, even though money is "made up," that doesn't mean it isn't important. Because everyone has agreed that money has value, it's generally the only way we can get goods and services today. That's why it's so important to understand how money and the economy work.

Facing the Facts

Today, a lot of monetary **transactions** are done through the internet. People still agree that the numbers in their bank account or on their credit card bill have value, even though many people never hold that money in their hands anymore.

Credit cards give people a way to buy things without carrying paper money. However, they must be used carefully to avoid **debt**.

When Prices Go Up

The value of money doesn't always stay the same. Inflation is when the prices for goods and services in an economy go up. This means something that cost $2 yesterday could cost $4 next month. People need more money to buy the same amount of stuff. This makes the value of the money go down.

A little bit of inflation—around 2 percent per year—is normal. However, when prices rise by a lot or rise very quickly, it can be very hard for people to afford things they need.

Facing the Facts

Between 2019 and 2022, the price of bikes went up 43 percent. This is because so many people bought bikes during the COVID-19 **pandemic** that they were almost impossible to find.

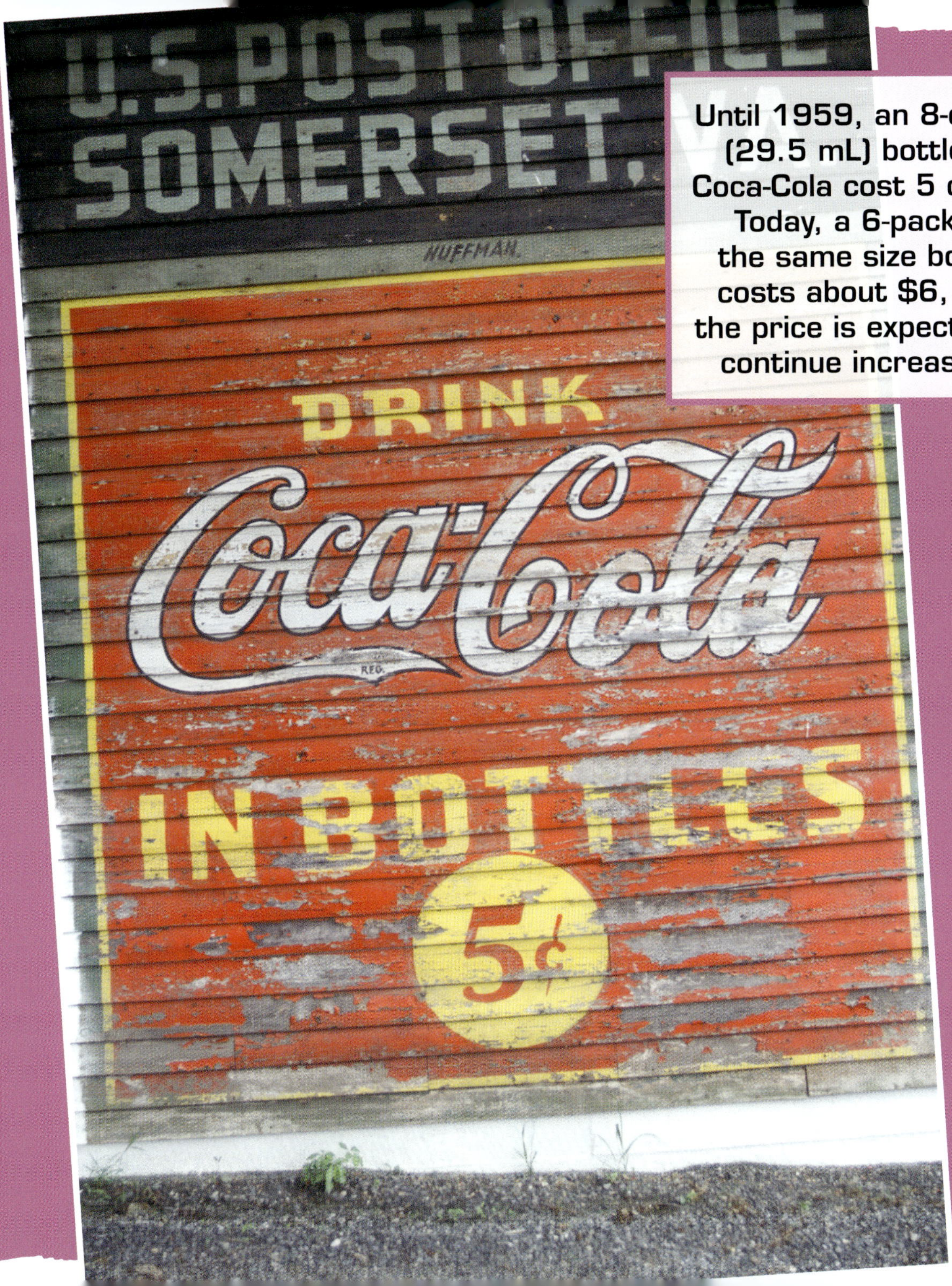

Until 1959, an 8-ounce (29.5 mL) bottle of Coca-Cola cost 5 cents. Today, a 6-pack of the same size bottle costs about $6, and the price is expected to continue increasing.

Everything Is Connected

There are a lot of reasons why prices go up more than expected. Often, these reasons are connected. For example, the price of a material used to make something might go up, so the price for the item also goes up. This can happen if the material becomes harder to find.

In 2021 and 2022, during the COVID-19 pandemic, people heard a lot about the global supply chain. This is the way goods are sent around the world. If there are problems at any point in the supply chain, prices go up. These problems can include longer wait times, higher shipping costs, and fewer workers.

Facing the Facts

During the COVID-19 pandemic, the cost of building supplies shot up. This was mainly because more people were staying home, and they were working on their homes to keep busy.

Food Supply Chain

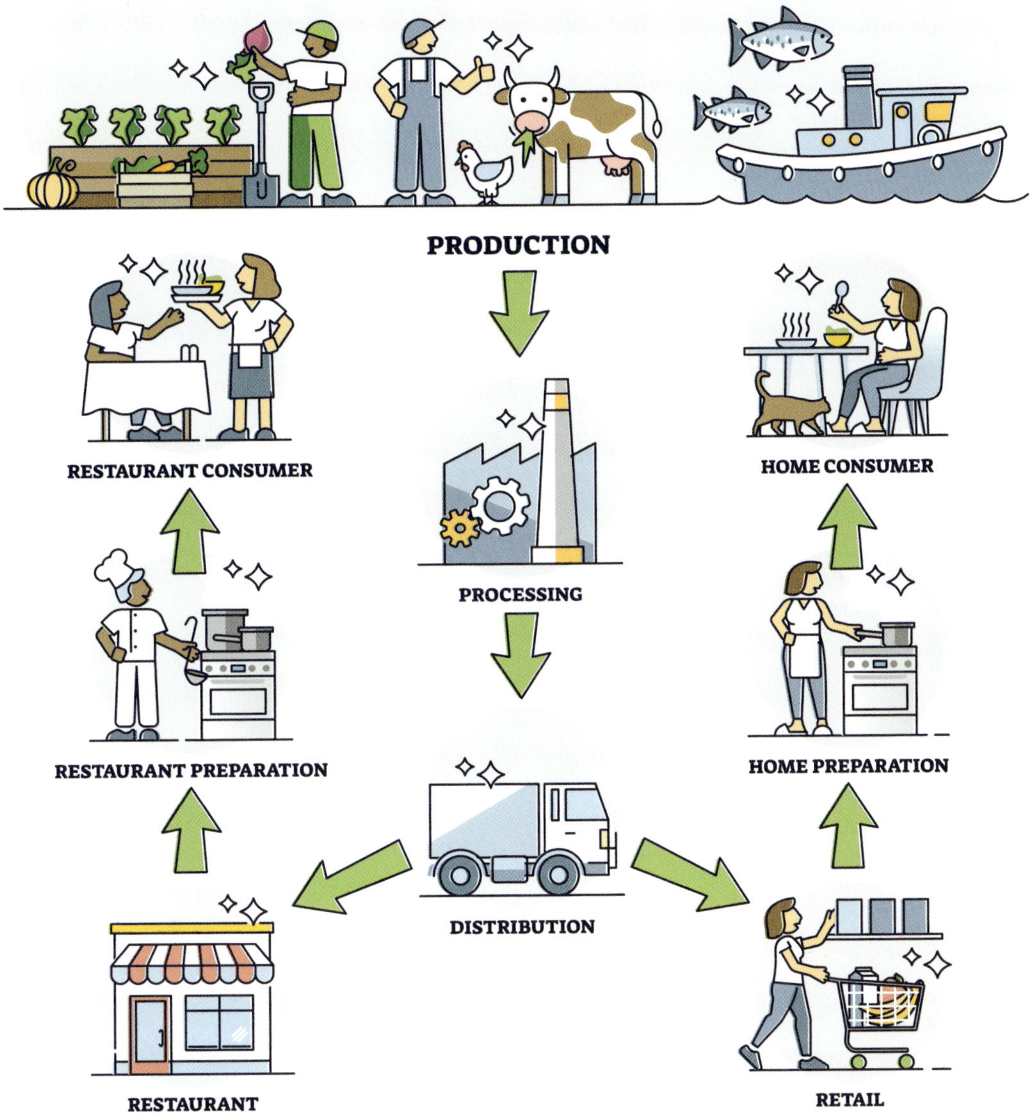

This shows how the supply chain works.

Cost-Push Inflation

When the global supply chain has problems, it can lead to a type of inflation called cost-push inflation. This happens when the supply of a good or service goes down, which makes prices go up. For example, in 2022, the United States had a sudden shortage of baby formula. Because of this, prices increased by about 14 percent. Formula was harder to find and more expensive to buy.

Natural **disasters** can also cause cost-push inflation by destroying factories or making it harder for people to deliver goods. Prices often go back down after the area hit by the natural disaster recovers.

Facing the Facts

A monopoly is when one company owns all of the supply of a good or service. Monopolies are illegal in part because they can cause cost-push inflation on purpose to make more money for the company.

Overfishing of some kinds of seafood, such as shrimp, is causing cost-push inflation.

Demand-Pull Inflation

Another kind of inflation is called demand-pull inflation. This is when the demand for a good or service goes up faster than the supply. When the economy is doing well, people have extra money to spend. This can cause demand for some goods and services to go up much faster than the supply can keep up with.

A part of the U.S. government called the Federal Reserve keeps careful track of the money supply. If it puts too much money into **circulation**, that can cause inflation. The Federal Reserve also has ways of slowing down inflation.

Facing the Facts

In many cases, inflation works itself out. When there's a shortage of goods, companies can often simply make more. When the shortage is fixed, the prices go back down. If that doesn't happen, the Federal Reserve steps in.

The mark of the Federal Reserve is on American paper money.

Bringing Inflation Down

One way the Federal Reserve can bring inflation down is with price controls. The government can set a minimum or maximum price on certain goods to make them more affordable. It can also use something called contractionary monetary **policy**. When something contracts, it gets smaller. This is the idea behind this policy.

Contractionary monetary policy increases interest rates. When people take out loans, they have to pay interest, which is extra money a lender charges a borrower. When the Federal Reserve raises interest rates, borrowing money becomes more expensive. This slows inflation because people borrow less money when interest is high.

Facing the Facts

High interest rates slow down the economy by lowering business activity. Companies' costs go up, so they hire fewer people. With fewer jobs, people have less money to spend, so prices go down.

People have to apply for a bank loan. The bank can decide not to lend to them if they don't have a good chance of paying back both the loan and the interest.

Hyperinflation

If inflation is not controlled, it can become hyperinflation. Hyperinflation is when the inflation rate is more than 50 percent per month. This is very bad for people because the cost of things they use every day—such as food and gasoline—rises very quickly. In very bad cases, the price of goods can go up daily.

Once hyperinflation gets going, it's very hard to stop. This is why governments generally pay close attention to inflation and try to fix it as soon as they can. Fortunately for citizens, hyperinflation isn't often a problem.

Facing the Facts

In 2022, inflation in the United States and the United Kingdom was the highest it had been in 40 years. However, neither country was experiencing hyperinflation.

Germany put out this 20,000-mark bill in 1923, when it was experiencing hyperinflation after World War I (1914–1918). At this time, 1 U.S. dollar was worth 1 trillion German marks.

How to Help

Inflation can seem scary and confusing. When people suddenly have trouble affording things they've never had trouble buying before, it's very upsetting. It's hard to know what to do when inflation starts to rise.

One important thing you can do is learn more about inflation and how it affects people. Understand that not every family has the same amount of money. If your family isn't feeling the effects of inflation, remember that other families are. Be **empathetic** to your friends and classmates if they have trouble paying for things.

Facing the Facts

Inflation became worse around the world when the president of Russia, Vladimir Putin, started a war in the nearby country of Ukraine in February 2022. This affected the global supply chain.

WHAT CAN YOU DO?

Buy from local small businesses instead of large companies so the money you spend stays in your community.

If you aren't feeling the effects of inflation, consider giving money or goods to groups that help people in need.

Read more about the economy so you know where your money comes from and where it goes.

Learn more about how inflation works and how it affects people.

Write to your government leaders if you have strong opinions about how they're handling inflation.

There are many things you can do when inflation starts to rise.

GLOSSARY

barter: To trade one thing for another without the use of money.

circulation: Passage from place to place or person to person.

debt: Something (usually money) owed to another.

disaster: Something such as a flood or a tornado that happens suddenly and causes much suffering or loss.

empathetic: Understanding and able to share the emotions and experiences of another person.

overfishing: Fishing so much that certain kinds of sea animals start to disappear.

pandemic: An occurrence in which a disease spreads quickly to multiple countries around the world at the same time and affects many people at once.

policy: A set of guidelines or rules that determine a course of action.

transaction: An exchange or transfer of goods, services, or money.

valuable: Having a lot of worth.

wampum: A type of money made of beads that was used by some Native American groups.

FOR MORE INFORMATION

WEBSITES

BrainPOP Jr: Economics
jr.brainpop.com/socialstudies/economics
Learn more about goods and services.

Kiddle: Inflation Facts for Kids
kids.kiddle.co/Inflation
This website takes a closer look at inflation.

BOOKS

Schuh, Mari C., and Keli Sipperley. *How Money Is Made.* Vero Beach, FL: Rourke Educational Media, 2019.

Sebree, Chet'la. *Understanding Inflation.* New York, NY: Cavendish Square, 2020.

Publisher's note to educators and parents: Our editors have carefully reviewed these websites to ensure that they are suitable for students. Many websites change frequently, however, and we cannot guarantee that a site's future contents will continue to meet our high standards of quality and educational value. Be advised that students should be closely supervised whenever they access the Internet.

INDEX